POEMS
for EVERYDAY PEOPLE

ILENA J. CRUSHSHON

Copyright © 2018 by Ilena J. Crushshon.

All rights reserved. No part of this publication may be reproduced, distributed, or transmitted in any form or by any means, including photocopying, recording, or other electronic or mechanical methods, without the prior written permission of the author, except in the case of brief quotations embodied in critical reviews and certain other noncommercial uses permitted by copyright law.

Printed in the United States of America

ISBN 13:   Paperback: 978-1-948172-30-1
            eBook: 978-1-948172-29-5

STONEWALL PRESS
PAVING YOUR WAY TO SUCCESS

Stonewall Press
363 Paladium Court
Owings Mills, MD 21117
www.stonewallpress.com
1-888-334-0980

Table of Contents

Foreword 1
Beautiful Words 3
Dreams 4
For Denise 5
Come Sunday 7
Angels of God 8
Ballad for Youth Gone Too Soon 9
Love 11
Ordinary People 12
Gone 13
The Gift of Love 15
Secrets 16
Tribute 17
Thank God! 19
Reflection 20
The Man of Music 21
Identity 23
Simple Gifts 24
Quest 25
Joy 27
The Promise 28
Stop the Violence 29
Time 31
Everyday Heroes 32
Today 33
Where Beauty Lives 35

Dedicated to my cousin,
Bill McClellan
The Legendary Man of Music, without whose inspiration, encouragement,
and faith this little book could not have been written.

And with gratitude to
LaSchelle,
the ultimate friend, who was always there to encourage and help me.

Thanks to you both!

Foreword

Welcome to my little book of *Poems for Everyday People*. Before you read its contents, I have a confession to make; I am not a poet! That's right. I'm a writer but I'm not a poet. How can that be, you may ask? It's simple. For one year God has awakened me at 3:15AM to give me a new poem, twenty-five in all.

At first, I tried to ignore the pithy little nuggets but it soon became clear these were not just poems. They were words of love, encouragement, peace, joy and inspiration spoken by God through me. They are a gift to his children, everyday people facing life's trials and tribulations.

Thank you God for choosing me as your voice.

Beautiful Words

Our lives are shaped
By the words we speak.
Words have power to build or destroy,
To inspire or discourage.

Words spoken in anger
Can never be taken back
The pain they inflict
Lives on in our secret place

Beautiful words of love and hope,
Comfort and joy
Are blessings to the speaker
And the receiver.

Dreams

Dreamers beware!
Be careful what you say.
The dream killers are waiting
To take your dream away.

A dream is a gift
Given by God above.
To bless the weary world
Wrapped in his tender love.

The dream killers wait in silence
Their evil work to do.
A look, a word, a snide remark
Must not discourage you.

Believe in your dream.
Cast out all doubt and fear.
Trust the Father within
Your dream will soon appear.

For Denise

Music is a gift
Given by God above
Bestowed on special people
Blessed by His everlasting love

The sounds of your music
Will echo through the halls
Reminding us of golden days
That brought pleasure to us all

And now, as you prepare to go
We just want you to know—
You are the gift
You are the music.

Come Sunday

Her hands are gnarled
Her back is bent
When she walks
Her steps are slow but sure

She concedes with quiet grace
To the changes wrought by time
No longer the vibrant girl
Whose aura filled a room

Alone she seeks to fill the days
With services to others
Kindness from a giving heart
A blessing in expression

But once a week
Her spirit soars
She wakes with words of joy
Come Sunday she'll be whole

Angels of God

Their love is unconditional
Their eyes, open and welcoming,
Are filled with trust and innocence.
Being with them offers unexpected delights.

In times of sadness,
They offer comforting arms,
A tiny hand to hold
A peace beyond understanding

The sound of their laughter
Is like bells pealing
Without them, life seems somehow empty.
If you want to see God, hug a child.

Ballad for Youth Gone Too Soon

I look in the mirror
And what do I see?
Eyes clouded with sadness
Staring back at me.

Where did she go,
That girl I used to know?
With a smile that warmed the heart
And a laugh like pealing bells

When did it all fade from sight
Vanishing like a thief in the night?
I turned around,
And it was gone.

Oh endless days of blue and gold
Sunsets tinged with orange
Purple nights filled with stars,
A story waiting to be told.

We cannot call it back,
It is forever gone.
Take one last look then close the door.
Somehow we must go on.

Love

You are love
Your smile brings sunshine
To a dark and dreary day

You are love
When life's trials threaten
You chase the fear away

You are love
In times of loss and sorrow
Your presence helps to ease the pain

You are love
I am love
We are love

Ordinary People

Most of us
Are ordinary people.
Living out our days
In ordinary ways.

We fight the fires
And nurse the sick.
Tend the land
And teach the young.

We build the bridges
And make the goods.
Protect the innocent
And so much more.

When crises come
And storm clouds gather,
We do not fold.
Our faith sustains us.

We are ordinary people,
Standing through the whirl.
We don't just move mountains;
We move the world!

Gone

I always knew the day would come
When you would no longer be there
Standing inside the door, smiling
Directing congregants as they arrived.

Your face, filled with kindness,
Captured my heart and lifted my spirits,
You smiled at me
And I began to dream.

Standing there, like an ebony god
Your presence overwhelmed me
Even though I knew you'd never love me
What if, I fantasized, what if?

And, now you're gone
With no forewarning or word of good-bye
And I am left to wonder,
What if? What if?

The Gift of Love

The love you are seeking
Is seeking you.
The dream you envision
Is waiting to unfold.

Love waits patiently
Its wonders to bestow.
On those whose hearts are open
And receptive to its call.

Love is the greatest
Gift of all.
It lifts us up
To what we're meant to be.

Secrets

Our secrets are revealed at night,
Alone in the dark,
While the night winds wail,
We take off our masks.

Our sins of omission and commission
Weigh heavily upon us.
We seek ways to make amends
And do better next time.

Naked before God and self,
We face the truth
That only we know.
We accept our own reality.

Our prayers pierce the silence
Offering penance for our redemption
A new day soon will come
And, once again, we will don our masks.

Tribute

I was sinking
I had lost my way
Storm clouds gathering everyday
Father God I prayed
Heal me, guide me, use me
So others may know your greatness

My prayer was answered
The day I heard your voice
Anointed one
Beloved of God
Your words fell like the thundering rain
Inspiring me to dream again

Thank God!

Did you thank God today?
When you woke up this morning
And saw the familiar surroundings
Did you thank Him?

Did you thank God today?
When the doctor gave you the diagnosis
But told you there was hope,
Did you thank Him?

Did you thank God today?
When flames engulfed the house
But you got out just before,
Did you thank Him?

Did you thank God today?
When you remembered the many times
His grace and mercy set you free
Did you thank Him?

Reflection

You are young; I am old
Your story is yet to unfold
What laurels will you bring to Rome?
What mountains will you climb?
Whose life, shattered and broken,
Will rise because of words you have spoken
What dreams, hidden, in the silence of night
Will your inspiration bring to light
I am old; You are young
We meet in the middle
Until our song is sung.

The Man of Music

The house lights rise
The curtains slowly part
As he takes the podium
The applause begins to build.

He raises his arms
The music begins
Each instrument at his command
Softly, slowly the melody fills the hall.

Arms moving easily through the air
His body sways in time with the music
A perfect blending of sight and sound
The legendary man of music.

IDENTITY

Who are you?
Do you know who you are?
When you stand before the mirror
Do you recognize the face staring back?

Beware the identity thieves they say
Can your identity be stolen?
Do you know who you are?
Do you know the "you" behind the mask?

Only in the silence,
Away from the chattering crowd,
Can you find the truth of you
And discover your identity.

Simple Gifts

We all have gifts
Big or little,
Large or small,
Our gifts are a work order from God.

Have you found your gift?
Do you know what it is?
Is yours the smile
That lifts the sad or lonely?
Is yours the voice
That reassures the meek and fearful?

Will your touch bring comfort
To one who grieves?
Will your life inspire
One who has lost his way?
Do your words affirm
The goodness that is God?

Discover your gift!
Let it shine!
It was not meant to be
Buried in the chaos of life.
Give your gift freely.
It will return to you
Blessed and multiplied.

Quest

Love is all around us
Waiting to be invited into our lives
It walks beside us silently
Seeking our recognition
Failing to receive it, it moves on.

We seek love's warmth and comfort,
Our eyes fixed on what lies ahead
Never looking to the right or left
Our quest is endlessly futile.
Where is our soul mate? We cry

The search continues
Through the noisome hurley burley
And the serenity and peace of nature
Dismayed, we abandon our quest
If only we had turned our heads.

Joy

Of all God's gifts,
Joy often eludes us.
We look for it in many places
But our quests seem to fail.

Are you looking for joy?
Have you seen the sunset lately?
Or watched children playing on the beach?
Does your cat curl up beside your feet?

Are you looking for joy?
Did your best friend's health suddenly return?
Was the bouquet of roses a surprise?
When have you last counted the stars?

Joy does not announce itself
It is always here, waiting
If we lift our eyes and open our minds
We will find it.

The Promise

Listen. Pay attention.
You who are weary,
You who are sick,
You who despair,
Listen.

I am in the rustling wind.
I am in the gentle rain.
In the silence of the night,
And the first blush of the dawn.
Listen.

You are not alone: I am by your side.
Rest your hand in mine.
I will be your guide.
I will see you through.
Just listen.

Stop the Violence

Tears
Falling from my eyes
Sliding down my face
Tears
Too many tears
Too many broken hearts
Stop the violence!

Tears
Hot salty tears
Sad, bitter tears
I cannot hold them back
I cannot make them stop
I cannot bear the pain
Stop the violence!

The cries of the fallen
Echo in my ears
The faces of their loved ones
Forever etched with tears
Why?
The question lingers in the air
Will the answer come too late?
Stop the violence!

Time

Time stands still
Arms outstretched, watching
As the parade of humankind passes by.

It is a disorderly procession
Full of chicanery and challenges
Only the strong of faith
Overcome its pitfalls.

The young and the old
The rich and the poor
The weak and the strong
The good and the bad

Each following destiny's winding path
As it twists and turns
Bringing expected and unexpected experiences
It is a never-ending spectacle.

Time stands still, watching.

Everyday Heroes

There are heroes among us
Ordinary people like you and me.
Unknown and unsung
Doers of deeds big and small.

They are there when someone needs them
Like angels from above
There to meet the challenge
Secure in His everlasting love.

A sudden screech
A distant sound
A cry for help
A problem to be solved

They cannot predict the moment
They may be called upon
To aid a fellow traveler
Whose journey has gone wrong.

They seek no glory
No praise, no reward.
There are heroes among us
The foot soldiers of the Lord.

Today

Nestled between yesterday and tomorrow
Today waits patiently
Open and filled with possibilities
Ready to fulfill our dreams

Yesterday is forever gone
We can never call it back
The love, the laughter, the tears
Are only memories now

Tomorrow is uncertain
A mystery waiting to unfold
Our hopes and dreams
Are hidden behind its veil

Today is the door to tomorrow
Well lived, it moves us toward our goals
There is promise in every moment
A story waiting to be told

Where Beauty Lives

The princess in her tower
The diva on the screen
The prom queen and her court
The model on the ramp

All are beautiful

The world pays homage to beauty
Knees bend
Music plays
Voices rise in adoration

But for those of us
Whom beauty passed by
Who sought to create its illusion
And reap its rewards

Somebody loved us
Looked beyond our imperfections
And saw the beauty within
After all, isn't that what love does?

www.ingramcontent.com/pod-product-compliance
Lightning Source LLC
Chambersburg PA
CBHW071549080526
44588CB00011B/1841